D1312038

Table of Contents

Table of Contents

Table of Contents

Name: _____

Comprehension: Snow Is Cold!

Directions: Read about snow. Circle the answers.

When you play in snow, dress warmly. Wear a coat. Wear a hat. Wear gloves. Do you wear these when you play in snow?

1. Snow is

        warm.

        cold.

2. When you play in snow, dress

        warmly.

        quickly.

Directions: List three things to wear when you play in snow.

_____

- -

_____

- -

_____

- -

Same and Different

Directions: Circle five things in picture #1 that are not in picture #2.

#1

#2

Name:

Sequencing: Make a Snowman!

Directions: Write the number of the sentence that goes with each picture in the box.

1. Roll a large snowball for the snowman's bottom.

2. Make another snowball and put it on top of the first.

3. Put the last snowball on top.

4. Dress the snowman.

Classifying: What Does Not Belong?

Directions: Circle the two things that do not belong in the picture.
Write why they do not belong.

1. _____

_____

_____

2. _____

_____

_____

Classifying: These Keep Me Warm

Directions: Color the things that keep you warm.

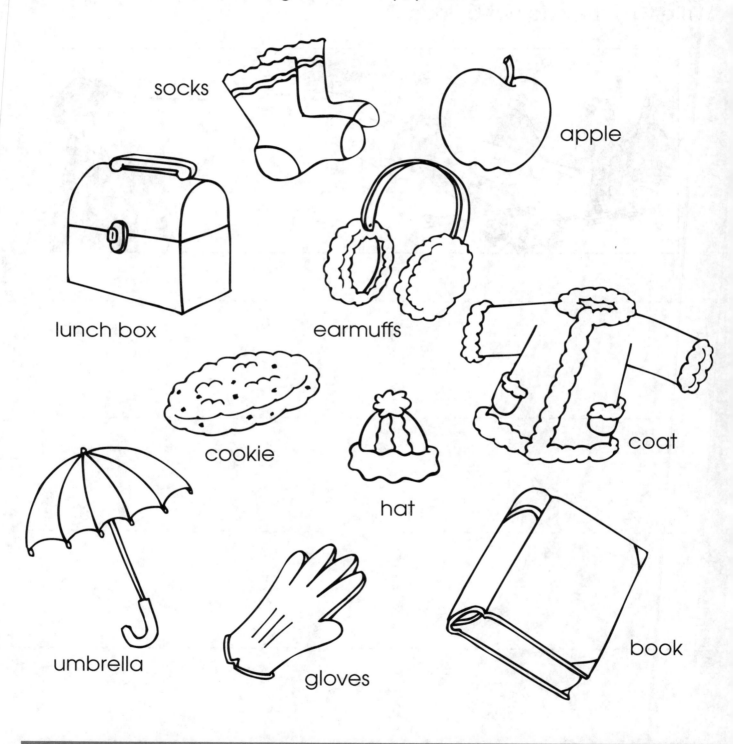

socks

apple

lunch box

earmuffs

coat

cookie

hat

umbrella

gloves

book

Comprehension: Raking Leaves

Directions: Read about raking leaves. Then answer the questions.

I like to rake leaves. Do you? Leaves die each year. They get brown and dry. They fall from the trees. Then we rake them up.

1. What color are leaves when they die?

   _____

   -

2. What happens when they die?

   -

   _____

   -

3. What do we do when leaves fall?

   _____

   -

Sequencing: Raking Leaves

Directions: Write a number in each box to show the order of the story.

Classifying: Leaves

Directions: Cut out the leaves. Put them into two groups. Glue each group in a box on the top of the page. Write a name for each group.

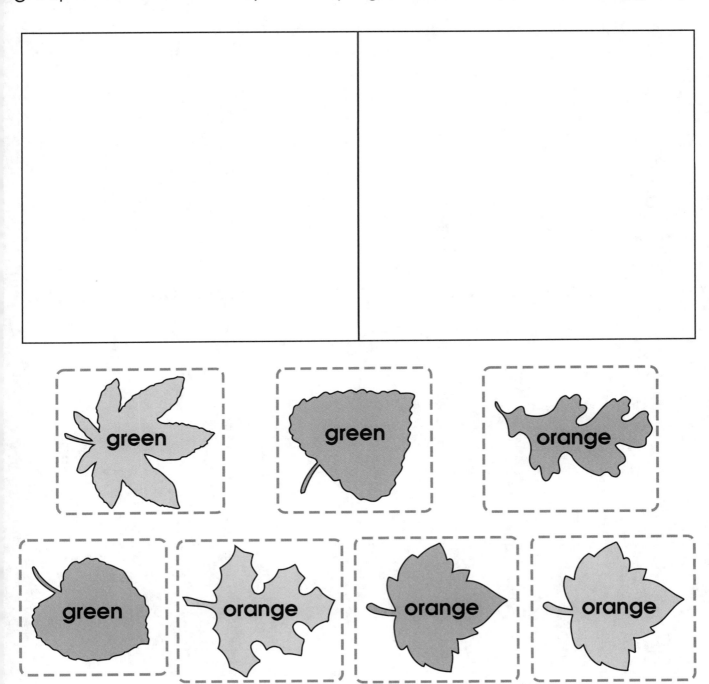

green

green

orange

green

orange

orange

orange

Page is blank for cutting exercise on previous page.

Name: _____

Comprehension: Growing Flowers

Directions: Read about flowers. Then write the answers.

   Some flowers grow in pots. Many flowers grow in flower beds. Others grow beside the road. Flowers begin from seeds. They grow into small buds. Then they open wide and bloom. Flowers are pretty!

1. Name two places flowers grow.

   -

   -

2. Flowers begin from

3. Then flowers grow into small

4. Flowers then open wide and

13

Flower Puzzle

Directions: Read the story about flowers again. Then complete the puzzle.

Across:

2. Flowers do this when they open wide.

3. Flowers grow from these.

Down:

1. A flower can grow in a flower bed or a ___.

2. Before they bloom, flowers grow ___.

Sequencing: How Flowers Grow

Directions: Read the story. Then write the steps to grow a flower.

   First find a sunny spot. Then plant the seed. Water it. The flower will start to grow. Pull the weeds around it. Remember to keep giving the flower water. Enjoy your flower.

1. _____ .

2. _____ .

3. _____ .

4. _____ .

5. _____ .

Name: _____

Review

Directions: Write words in the blanks to make a label for a seed packet. Use ideas from the stories on pages 13 and 15 and your own ideas.

_____

- -

_____ Seeds

Plant seeds in a
_____

- -

_____ .

Give them lots of
_____

- -

_____ .

A bud will grow. Then it will
_____

- -

_____ .

The flower will keep growing if you pull the
_____

- -

_____ around it.

- -

Your flowers will be very _____ .

Name: _____

Review

Directions: Read the story and look at the pictures. Then write the answers.

Some clothes are for winter. Some clothes are for summer. Winter clothes keep us warm. Summer clothes keep us cool. In summer, I put on shorts, then a shirt and then sandals. These clothes keep me cool!

shirt   scarf   coat   hat   sandals   shorts

1. Tell the order of clothes I put on in summer.

--------------------   --------------------   --------------------

First   Then   Last

2. List the winter clothes pictured.

--------------------   --------------------   --------------------

3. How are summer and winter clothes different?

Summer clothes keep us   Winter clothes keep us

--------------------   --------------------

Name: _____

Comprehension: Balloons

Directions: Read the story. Then answer the questions.

Some balloons float. They are filled with gas. Some do not float. They are filled with air. Some clowns carry balloons. Balloons come in many colors. What color do you like?

1. What makes balloons float?

2. What is in balloons that do not float?

3. What shape are the balloons the clown is holding?

Name: _____

Comprehension: Balloons

Directions: Read the story about balloons again. Draw a picture for the sentence in each box.

The clown is holding red, yellow and blue balloons filled with air.

The clown is holding purple, orange, green and blue balloons filled with gas.

Name: _____

Same and Different: Clowns

Directions: Look at the two clowns. Color the things in picture #2 that are different from the things in picture #1.

#1

#2

Name: _____

Following Directions: Color the Clown

Directions: Color the clown. Use your crayons this way: 1 = red, 2 = blue, 3 = orange, 4 = pink.

Directions: Write the answers on the lines.

1. What color did you use for the clown's hair?

- -

2. What color is the clown's nose?

- -

3. What color is the clown's collar?

- -

4. What color is the clown's mouth?

- -

Classifying: Clowns and Balloons

Some words describe clowns. Some words describe balloons.

Directions: Read the words. Write the words that match in the correct columns.

float	laughs	hat	string
air	feet	pop	nose

clown

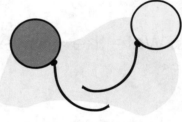

balloons

Sequencing: Petting a Cat

Directions: Read the story. Then write the answers.

Do you like cats? I do. To pet a cat, move slowly. Hold out your hand. The cat will come to you. Then pet its head. Do not grab a cat! It will run away.

To pet a cat . . .

1. Move _____ .

2. Hold our your _____ .

3. The cat will come to _____ .

4. Pet the cat's _____ .

5. Do not _____ a cat!

Comprehension: Cats

Directions: Read the story about cats again. Then write the answers.

1. What is a good title for the story?

   _____

   -

   -

2. The story tells you how to - .

3. What part of your body should you pet a cat with?

   -

4. Why should you move slowly to pet a cat?

   -

   _____

5. Why do you think a cat will run away if you grab it?

   -

   - .

Name: _____

Comprehension: Cats

Directions: Look at the pictures and read about four cats. Then write the correct name beside each cat.

Fluffy, Blackie and Tiger are playing. Tom is sleeping. Blackie has spots. Tiger has stripes.

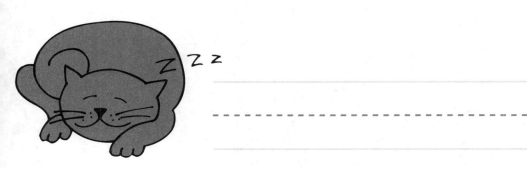

Same and Different: Cats

Directions: Compare the picture of the cats on page 25 to this picture. Write a word from the box to tell what is different about each cat.

purple ball	green bow	blue brush	red collar

1. Tom is wearing a _____ .

2. Blackie has a _____ .

3. Fluffy is wearing a _____ .

4. Tiger has a _____ .

Name: _____

Comprehension: Tigers

Directions: Read about tigers. Then write the answers.

Tigers sleep during the day. They hunt at night. Tigers eat meat. They hunt deer. They like to eat wild pigs. If they cannot find meat, tigers will eat fish.

1. When do tigers sleep?

----

2. Name two things tigers eat.

----

3. When do tigers hunt?

Name: _____

Following Directions: Tiger Puzzle

Directions: Read the story about tigers again. Then complete the puzzle.

Across:

1. When tigers cannot get meat, they eat_____ .

3. The food tigers like best is _____ .

4. Tigers like to eat this meat: wild _____ .

Down:

2. Tigers do this during the day.

Following Directions: Draw a Tiger

Directions: Follow directions to complete the picture of the tiger.

1. Draw black stripes on the tiger's body and tail.

2. Color the tiger's tongue red.

3. Draw claws on the feet.

4. Draw a black nose and two black eyes on the tiger's face.

5. Color the rest of the tiger orange.

6. Draw tall, green grass for the tiger to sleep in.

Name: _____

Review

Directions: Read about skiing. Circle the answers. Write a number in each box to show the order of the story.

Skiing Is Fun

You need to dress warmly to ski. One ski fits on each boot. You wear the skis to a chair called a ski lift. It takes you up in the air to a hill. When you get off, you ski down the hill. Be careful! Sometimes you will fall.

1. To ski, you need

two skis.

one ski.

2. Skiing is an

indoor sport.

outdoor sport.

Name: _____

Comprehension: Apples

Directions: Read about apples. Then write the answers.

I like  . Do you?   Some  are red.

Some  are green.   Some  are yellow.

1. How many kinds of apples does the story tell about?

- -

2. Name the kinds of apples.

- -

3. What kind of apple do you like best?

- -

Name: _____

Classifying: Fruit

Fruit tastes good. It is sweet! Fruit is a good snack.

Directions: Look at the words and pictures. Then write the names of the fruits in the blanks.

apple

banana

grapes

potato

orange

carrot

broccoli

Name: _____

Classifying: Vegetables

Vegetables grow in gardens. Vegetables help keep us healthy.

Directions: Look at the pictures. Then write the name of the vegetables in the blanks.

bread

beans

_ _

_ _

banana

lettuce

_ _

noodles

carrot

_ _

Add the name of one
more vegetable.

peas

_ _

broccoli

Comprehension: How We Eat

Directions: Read the story. Use words from the box to answer the questions.

   People eat with spoons and forks. They use a spoon to eat soup and ice cream. They use a fork to eat potatoes. They use a knife to cut their meat. They say, "Thank you. It was good!" when they finish.

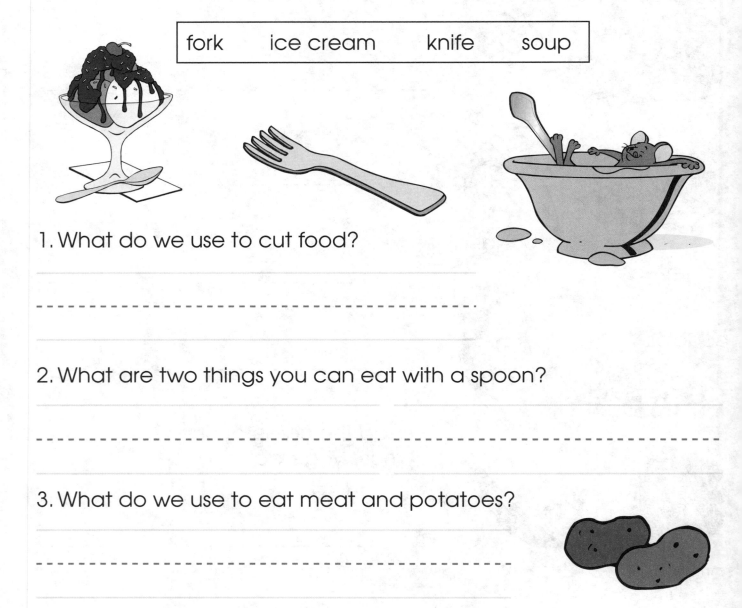

| fork | ice cream | knife | soup |

1. What do we use to cut food?

_____

- -

2. What are two things you can eat with a spoon?

_____

-   -

3. What do we use to eat meat and potatoes?

_____

- -

Classifying: Foods

Directions: Read the questions under each plate. Draw three foods on each plate to answer the questions.

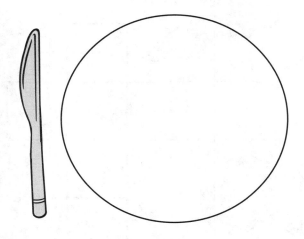

1. What foods can you cut with a knife?

2. What foods should you eat with a fork?

3. What foods can you eat with a spoon?

Name: _____

Comprehension: Familiar Objects

Directions: Write each word next to its picture in the puzzle.

bag

bird

1.

3.

2.

4.

apple

cookie

Directions: Complete the sentences. Write the answers in the blanks.

5. I can carry things in a _____ .

6. I like to eat a red _____

_____

7. I wish I could fly like a _____ .

8. I can bake a _____ .

Name: _____

Classifying: Things That Belong Together

Directions: Circle the pictures in each row that belong together.

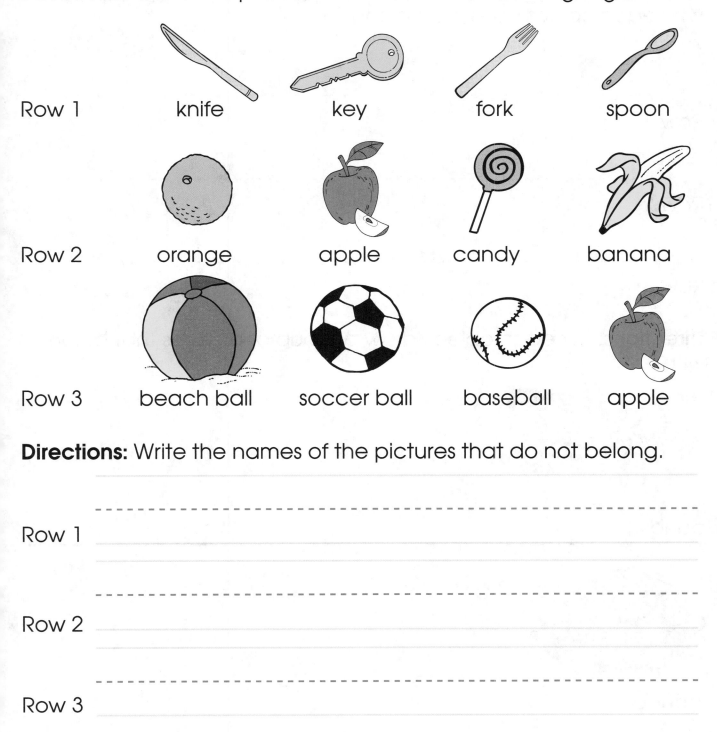

Row 1   knife   key   fork   spoon

Row 2   orange   apple   candy   banana

Row 3   beach ball   soccer ball   baseball   apple

Directions: Write the names of the pictures that do not belong.

Row 1

Row 2

Row 3

Classifying: Why They Are Different

Directions: Look at your answers on page 37. Write why each object does not belong.

Row 1 _____

_____

Row 2 _____

_____

Row 3 _____

Directions: For each object, draw a group of pictures that belong with it.

candy bar

_____

lettuce

Comprehension: Write a Party Invitation

Directions: Read about the party. Then complete the invitation.

The party will be at Dog's house. The party will start at 1:00 P.M. It will last 2 hours. Write your birthday for the date of the party.

Party Invitation

Where: _____

Date: _____

Time It Begins: _____

Time It Ends: _____

_____

Directions: On the last line, write something else about the party.

Name: _____

Sequencing: Pig Gets Ready

Directions: Number the pictures of Pig getting ready for the party to show the order of the story.

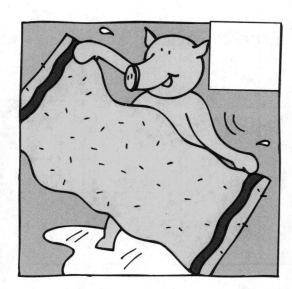

What kind of party do you think Pig is going to?

_____

Name: _____

Comprehension: An Animal Party

Directions: Use the picture for clues. Write words from the box to answer the questions.

bear	cat
dog	elephant
giraffe	hippo
pig	tiger

1. Which animals have bow ties?

_____

- -

_____

2. Which animal has a hat?

- -

- -

3. Which animal has a striped shirt?

Classifying: Party Items

Directions: Draw a ☐ around objects that are food for the party. Draw a △ around the party guests. Draw a ◯ around the objects used for fun at the party.

ice cream

candy

games

tiger

noise makers

cake

garbage can

cat

hat

glasses

candle

bear

juice

balloons

giraffe

pig

potato chips

hippo

Name: _____

Review

Directions: Read about cookies. Then write your answers.

Cookies are made with many things. All cookies are made with flour. Some cookies have nuts in them. Some cookies do not. Some cookies have chocolate chips. Some do not. Cookbooks give directions on how to make cookies.

First, turn on the oven. Then get out all the things that go in the cookies. Mix them together. Roll them out, and cut the cookies. Bake the cookies. Now eat them!

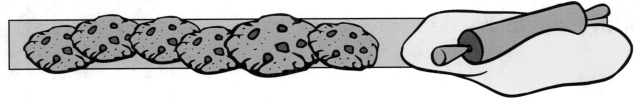

1. Tell one way all cookies are the same.

- -

2. Name one different thing in cookies.

- -

3. Where do you find directions for making cookies?

- -

Name: _____

Comprehension: The Teddy Bear Song

Do you know the Teddy Bear Song? It is very old!

Directions: Read the Teddy Bear Song. Then answer the questions.

Teddy bear, teddy bear, turn around.

Teddy bear, teddy bear, touch the ground.

Teddy bear, teddy bear, climb upstairs.

Teddy bear, teddy bear, say your prayers.

Teddy bear, teddy bear, turn out the light.

Teddy bear, teddy bear, say, "Good night!"

1. What is the first thing the teddy bear does?

- -

2. What is the last thing the teddy bear does?

- -

3. What would you name a teddy bear?

- -

Name:

Following Directions: Make a Teddy Bear

Directions: Color and cut out the teddy bear. Act out the song on page 44 with your teddy bear.

Page is blank for cutting exercise on previous page.

Comprehension: A New Teddy Bear Song

Directions: Write words to make a new teddy bear song. Act out your new song with your teddy bear as you read it.

_____

Teddy bear, teddy bear, turn _____ .

_____

Teddy bear, teddy bear, touch the _____ .

_____

Teddy bear, teddy bear, climb _____ .

_____

Teddy bear, teddy bear, turn out _____ .

_____

Teddy bear, teddy bear, say, _____ .

Name: _____

Sequencing: Put Teddy Bear to Bed

Directions: Read the song about the teddy bear again. Write a number in each box to show the order of the story.

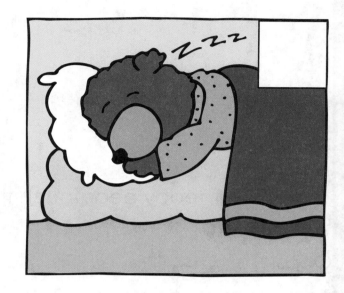

Name: _____

Comprehension: Play Simon Says

Directions: Read how to play Simon Says. Then answer the questions.

SIMON SAYS, CLAP YOUR HANDS!

Simon Says

Here is how to play Simon Says: One kid is Simon. Simon is the leader. Everyone must do what Simon says and does but only if the leader says, "Simon says" first. Let's try it. "Simon says, 'Pat your head.'" "Simon says, 'Pat your nose. Pat your toes.'"

Oops! Did you pat your toes? I did not say, "Simon says," first. If you patted your toes, you are out!

1. Who is the leader in this game? -

2. What must the leader say first each time? -

3. What happens if you do something and the leader did not say, "Simon says?" -

Comprehension: Play Simon Says

Directions: Read each sentence. Look at the picture next to it. Circle the picture if the person is playing Simon Says correctly.

1. Simon says, "Put your hands on your hips."

2. Simon says, "Stand on one leg."

3. Simon says, "Put your hands on your head."

4. Simon says, "Ride a bike."

5. Simon says, "Jump up and down."

6. Simon says, "Pet a dog."

7. Simon says, "Make a big smile."

Following Directions: Play Simon Says

Directions: Read the sentences. If Simon tells you to do something, follow the directions. If Simon does not tell you to do something, go to the next sentence.

1. Simon says: Cross out all the numbers 2 through 9.

2. Simon says: Cross out the vowel that is in the word "sun."

3. Cross out the letter "B."

4. Cross out the vowels "A" and "E."

5. Simon says: Cross out the consonants in the word "cup."

6. Cross out the letter "Z."

7. Simon says: Cross out all the "K's."

8. Simon says: Read your message.

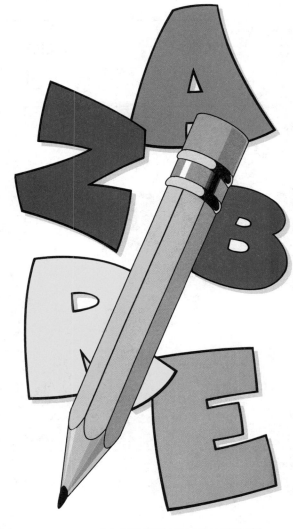

C 3 G U 7 P R U C P E K C P A 8 K K

6 T P U P J C 5 P O K 9 P B U P K K

Name: _____

Same and Different: Look at Simon

Directions: Find four things in picture #2 that are not in picture #1. Write your answers. Use words from the box.

hat	head	socks	bare feet
feather	watch	untied shoes	shirt

1. _____

2. _____

3. _____

4. _____

Comprehension: Crayons

Directions: Read about crayons. Then write your answers.

Crayons come in many colors.
Some crayons are dark colors.
Some crayons are light colors.
All crayons have wax in them.

1. How many colors of crayons are there?   many

    few

2. Crayons come in _____ colors

    and _____ colors.

3. What do all crayons have in them?

    _____

Name: _____

Following Directions: Hidden Picture

Directions: To find the hidden picture, color only the shapes with a number inside.

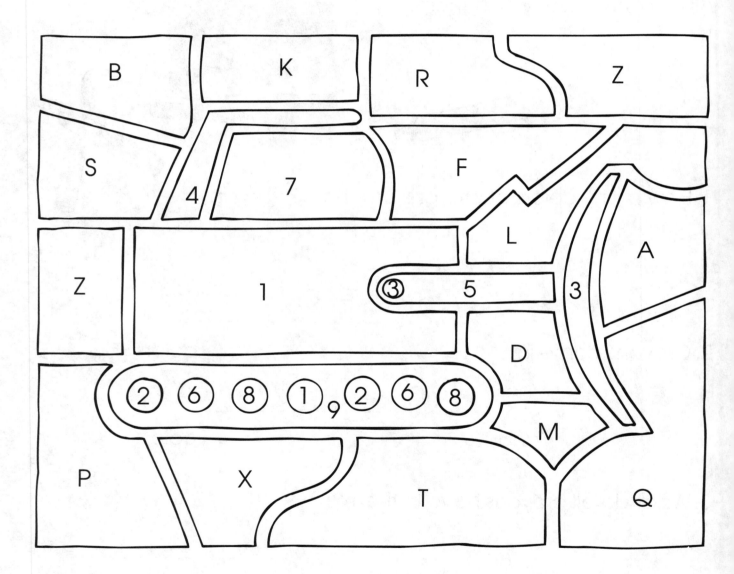

Name: _____

Comprehension: Rhymes

Directions: Read about words that rhyme. Then circle the answers.

Words that rhyme have the same end sounds. "Wing" and "sing" rhyme. "Boy" and "toy" rhyme. "Dime" and "time" rhyme. Can you think of other words that rhyme?

1. Words that rhyme have the same   end sounds.

                                   end letters.

TREE, SEE
SHOE, BLUE
KITE, BITE
MAKE, TAKE
FLY, BUY

2. "Time" rhymes with   "tree."

                             "dime."

Directions: Write one rhyme for each word.

wing   boy

- -

dime   pink

- -

Name:

Classifying: Rhymes

Directions: Circle the pictures in each row that rhyme.

Row 1   

Row 2   

Row 3   

Directions: Write the names of the pictures that do not rhyme.

These words do not rhyme:

      Row 1   Row 2   Row 3

--------------------   --------------------   --------------------

Classifying: Rhymes

Directions: Cut out the pieces. Read the words. Find two words that rhyme. Put the words together.

kite

my

tree

bell

buy

bee

well

white

Page is blank for cutting exercise on previous page.

Name: _____

Review

Directions: Read about ways you move. Circle the correct answer.

You can move in many ways. You can run. When you run, one foot hits the ground at a time. You can jump. When you jump, you land on two feet. You can hop. To hop, first stand on one leg. Then jump up and down.

1. Running and jumping are different because

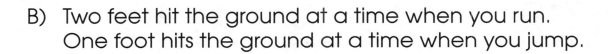

A) One foot hits the ground at a time
   when you run. Two feet hit the ground
   at a time when you jump.

OR

B) Two feet hit the ground at a time when you run.
   One foot hits the ground at a time when you jump.

Directions: Write directions on how to hop.

_____

2. First, _____ .

_____

3. Then, _____ .

Name: _____

Comprehension: Babies

Directions: Read about babies. Then write the answers.

Babies are small. Some babies cry a lot. They cry when they are wet. They cry when they are hungry. They smile when they are dry. They smile when they are fed.

1. Name two reasons babies cry.

_____ _____

2. Name two reasons babies smile.

_____ _____

3. Write a baby's name you like.

_____

Name: _____

Comprehension: Babies

Directions: Read each sentence. Draw a picture of a baby's face in the box to show if she would cry or smile.

1. The baby needs to have her diaper changed.

| 1 |

2. The baby has not eaten for awhile.

| 2 |

3. Dad put a dry diaper on the baby.

| 3 |

4. The baby is going to finish her bottle.

| 4 |

5. The baby finished her food but is still hungry.

| 5 |

Name: _____

Sequencing: Feeding Baby

Directions: Read the sentences. Write a number in each box to show the order of the story.

The baby smiles.

Mom makes the baby's food.

The baby is put in his chair.

The baby is crying.

Mom feeds the baby.

Name: _____

Same and Different: Compare the Twins

Directions: Read the story. Then use the words in the box and the picture to write your answers.

Ben and Ann are twin babies. They were born at the same time. They have the same mother. Ben is a boy baby. Ann is a girl baby.

mother	bow	boy	girl	hat	twins

1. Tell one way Ann and Ben are the same.

   _____

   _____

2. Anna and Ben are _____ .

3. Tell two ways Ann and Ben are different.

4. Ann is a _____ . Ben is _____ .

5. Ann is wearing a _____ . Ben is wearing a _____ .

Name: _____

Comprehension: Hats

Directions: Read about hats. Then write your answers.

There are many kinds of hats. Some baseball hats have brims. Some fancy hats have feathers. Some knit hats pull down over your ears. Some hats are made of straw. Do you like hats?

1. Name four kinds of hats.

-------------------------------   -------------------------------

-------------------------------   -------------------------------

-------------------------------   -------------------------------

Directions: Circle the correct answers.

2. What kind of hats pull down over your ears?

    straw hats

    knit hats

3. What are some hats made of?

    straw

    mud

Sequencing: Choosing a Hat

Directions: Write a number in each box to show the order of the story.

Classifying: Hats

Directions: A store has four types of hats. Draw three hats for each type listed. Write what kind of hats you think should be in the last group, and draw three of that kind.

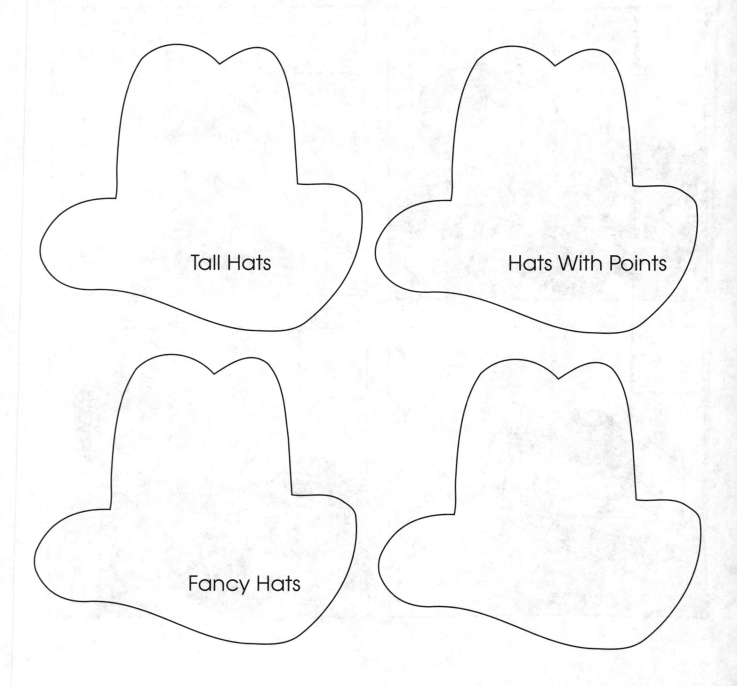

Tall Hats

Hats With Points

Fancy Hats

Classifying: Mr. Lincoln's Hat

Abraham Lincoln wore a tall hat. He liked to keep things in his hat so he would not lose them.

Directions: Cut out the pictures of things Mr. Lincoln could have kept in his hat. Glue those pictures on the hat.

letters	candle	 penny	one dollar
bowl	cat	watch	paper

Page is blank for cutting exercise on previous page.

Following Directions: Draw Hats

Directions: Draw a hat on each person. Read the sentences to know what kind of hat to draw.

1. The first girl is wearing a purple hat with feathers.

2. The boy next to the girl with the purple hat is wearing a red baseball hat.

3. The first boy is wearing a yellow knit hat.

4. The last boy is wearing a brown top hat.

5. The girl next to the boy with the red hat is wearing a blue straw hat.

Review

Directions: Read the story. Then circle the pictures of things that are wet.

Some things used in baking are dry. Some things used in baking are wet. To bake a cake, first mix the salt, sugar and flour. Then add the egg. Now, add the milk. Stir. Put the cake in the oven.

Directions: Tell the order to mix things when you bake a cake.

1. _____   4. _____

2. _____   5. _____

3. _____

Directions: Circle the answers.

6. The first things to mix are   dry.   wet.

7. Where are cakes baked?   oven   grill

Name: _____

Following Directions: Complete the Puzzle

Directions: Read the story. Then complete the puzzle.

The Zoo and the Farm

The zoo is for wild animals. Tigers live at the zoo. Some snakes live at the zoo. The farm is for tame animals. Ducks and donkeys live on farms.

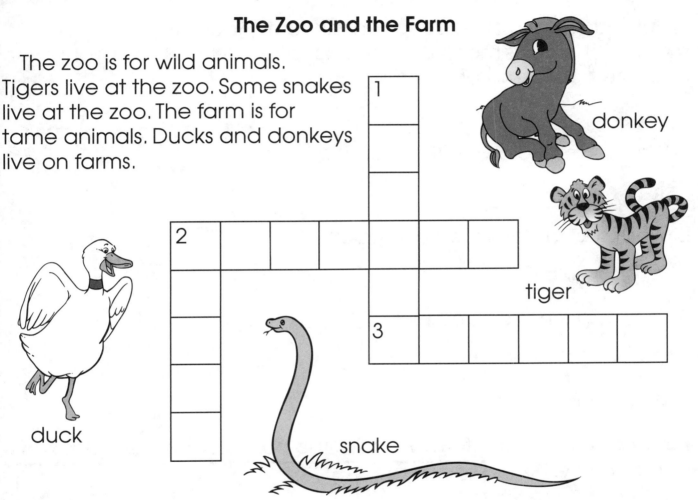

donkey

tiger

snake

duck

Across:

2. These animals say "hee-haw." They live on the farm.

3. These animals are long and thin. Some live in the zoo.

Down:

1. These animal have stripes. They live in the zoo.

2. These animals say "quack." They live on the farm.

Name: _____

Comprehension: Farm Sounds

Directions: Read the story. Then answer the questions.

You can hear many sounds on the farm. Roosters crow in the morning. The cows moo, and donkeys say, "hee-haw." You might even hear the tractor motor humming.

1. What animal crows in the morning?

2. What sound does the cow make?

3. This thing is not an animal?

4. What animal says "hee-haw"?

Directions: Circle the farm words in the puzzle. Look up and down and sideways.

donkey	a	l	b	x	m	d	y
	e	u	m	p	o	o	a
moo	k	c	f	h	o	n	j
rooster	q	k	t	u	l	k	w
tractor	r	o	o	s	t	e	r
	c	e	n	o	s	y	v
	t	r	a	c	t	o	r

Same and Different: Compare the Barnyards

Directions: Look at the pictures of the barnyards. Color the five things in picture #1 that are different from picture #2.

#1

#2

Name: _____

Comprehension: Animals

Directions: Read about inside and outside animals. Circle the pictures of animals that can live inside.

Some animals belong inside. Some animals belong outside. Wild animals belong outside. Large animals belong outside. Small, tame animals can live inside.

Directions: Write the names of animals that belong outside.

1. _____

2. _____

3. _____

4. _____

tiger

parakeets

ostrich

cat

horse

cow

Name: _____

Comprehension: Days

Directions: Read about the days of the week. Then answer the questions.

Do you know the names of the seven days of the week? Here they are: Sunday, Monday, Tuesday, Wednesday, Thursday, Friday and Saturday.

1. What day comes after Thursday?

_____

2. What day comes before Tuesday?

_____

3. How many days are in each week?

_____

Name: _____

Following Directions: Days of the Week

Calendars show the days of the week in order. Sunday comes first. Saturday comes last. There are five days in between. An **abbreviation** is a short way of writing words. The abbreviations for the days of the week are usually the first three or four letters of the word followed by a period.

Example: Sunday — Sun.

Directions: Write the days of the week in order on the calendar. Use the abbreviations.

Day 1	Day 2	Day 3
Sunday **Sun.**	Monday	Tuesday **Tues.**
Day 4	**Day 5**	**Day 6**
Wednesday	Thursday **Thurs.**	Friday
	Day 7 Saturday	

Name: _____

Comprehension: Boats

Directions: Read about boats. Then answer the questions.

See the boats! They float on water. Some boats have sails. The wind moves the sails. It makes the boats go. Many people name their sailboats. They paint the name on the side of the boat.

1. What makes sailboats move?

_____

_____

2. Where do sailboats float?

_____

_____

3. What would you name a sailboat?

_____

_____

Same and Different: Color the Boats

Directions: Find the three boats that are alike. Color them all the same. One boat is different. Color it differently.

Name: _____

Comprehension: A Boat Ride

Directions: Write a sentence under each picture to tell what is happening. Read the story you wrote.

- -

- -

- -

- -

Comprehension: Travel

Directions: Read the story. Then answer the questions.

Let's Take a Trip!

Pack your bag. Shall we go by car, plane or train? Let's go to the sea. When we get there, let's go on a sailboat.

1. What are three ways to travel?

   -

2. Where will we go?

   -

3. What will we do when we get there?

   -

Name: _____

Following Directions: Draw a Path

Directions: Read about how to get to the beach. Use a crayon to draw the way to the beach.

Let's Go to the Beach

On the way to the beach, you will stop for food, then gas. Next, you cross a bridge. Finally, you will be at the beach!

Review

Directions: Read the story. Then write the answers.

Fun With Balls

Some balls are soft. A beach ball is soft. Some balls are hard. We play baseball with a hard ball. Basketballs bounce. Can you throw a basketball through a hoop? First, bounce it three times. Then hold the basketball high. Now, throw it toward the hoop. Did you make a basket?

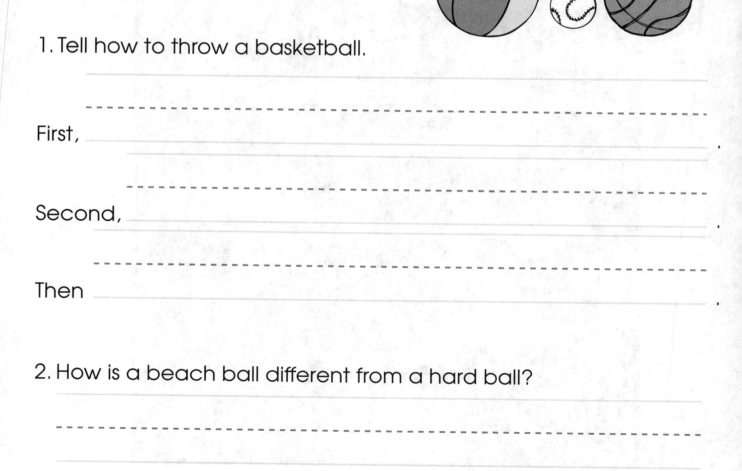

1. Tell how to throw a basketball.

_____

First, _____.

_____

Second, _____.

_____

Then _____.

2. How is a beach ball different from a hard ball?

_____

_____

Name: _____

Comprehension: Clocks

Directions: Read about clocks. Then answer the questions.

Ticking Clocks

Many clocks make two sounds. The sounds are tick and tock. Big clocks often make loud tick-tocks. Little clocks often make quiet tick-tocks. Sometimes people put little clocks in a box with a new puppy. The puppy likes the sound. The tick-tock makes the puppy feel safe.

1. What two sounds do many clocks make?

_____ and _____

2. What kind of tick-tocks do big clocks make?

_____

3. What kind of clock makes a new puppy feel safe?

_____

Sequencing: Help the Puppy Feel Safe

Directions: Read the story about clocks again. Then write a number in each box to show the order of the story.

Name: _____

Same and Different: These Don't Belong

Directions: Circle the pictures in each row that go together.

Row 1   cookies   cake   beans   ice cream

Row 2   apple   banana   orange   cookies

Row 3   kite   dice   checkers   chess

Directions: Write the names of the things that do not belong.

Row 1 _____

Row 2 _____

Row 3 _____

85

Classifying: Things to Drink

Directions: Circle the pictures of things you can drink. Write the names of those things in the blanks.

milk

ice

soup and crackers

juice

soda

ice-cream bar

Name: _____

Classifying: Things to Chew

Directions: Draw a line from the pictures of things you chew to the plate.

soup

ice-cream bar

pizza

carrot

soda

GULP!

macaroni

corn on the cob

milk

gum

Comprehension: Soup

Directions: Read about soup. Then write the answers.

I Like Soup

Soup is good! It is good for you, too. We eat most kinds of soup hot. Some people eat cold soup in the summer. Carrots and beans are in some soups. Do you like crackers with soup?

1. Name two ways people eat soup.

---------------------------------   -------------------------------------

_____   _____

2. Name two things that are in some soups.

---------------------------------   -------------------------------------

_____   _____

3. Name the kind of soup you like best.

_____

Same and Different: Soup

Directions: Circle the five things in picture #1 that are not in picture #2.

#1

#2

Comprehension: The Three Bears

Directions: Read about the three bears. Put #1 beside Papa Bear's bed. Put #2 beside Mama Bear's bed. Put #3 beside Baby Bear's bed.

The Three Bears

Do you know the story of the three bears? Papa Bear is the biggest bear. He has the biggest bed. Mama Bear is a middle-size bear. She has a middle-size bed. Baby Bear is the little bear. He has the smallest bed.

1

2

3

Name: _____

Comprehension: The Three Bears

Directions: Draw the objects that belong to the three bears. Then complete the sentences.

Draw the bowls.

Baby	Mama	Papa

Mama's bowl is _____ than Papa's.

Mama's bowl is _____ than Baby's.

Draw the chairs.

Papa	Mama	Baby

Papa's chair is _____ than Baby's.

Baby's chair is _____ than Mama's.

Name: _____

Following Directions: Three Bears Puzzle

Directions: Read the story about the three bears again. Then complete the puzzle.

Across:

1. Papa Bear is the _____ bear.

3. All the bears sleep in _____ .

Down:

1. This bear is the little bear.

2. Mama Bear is the middle-_____ bear.

Name: _____

Review

Directions: Read how to make no-cook candy. Then answer the questions.

Some candy needs to be cooked on a stove. You do not need to cook this kind of candy. It is easy to make. You will need a large bowl for mixing. You will need five things to make this candy.

> **No-Cook Candy**
>
> $\frac{1}{2}$ cup peanut butter
>
> 4 cups powdered sugar
>
> 1 cup cocoa
>
> pinch of salt
>
> 4 tablespoons milk
>
> Mix everything in the bowl. Roll it into small balls. (A pinch of salt is just a tiny bit.)

1. What is third on the list of things needed?

_____

- -

2. What is different about no-cook candy?

_____

- -

Directions: Write what to do to make no-cook candy.

3. First, mix everything in a bowl. Then.

_____

- -

_____

Name: _____

Comprehension: "Humpty Dumpty"

Directions: Read the poem. Draw a picture of Humpty Dumpty after he fell off the wall.

Humpty Dumpty sat on a wall.

Humpty Dumpty had a great fall.

All the king's horses and all the king's men

Couldn't put Humpty together again.

Sequencing: Put Humpty Together

Directions: Cut out the pieces and mix them up. Then read the sentence on each piece to put Humpty back together.

Humpty was sitting on a wall.

Humpty fell off the wall.

The king's horses and men tried to put Humpty together.

Humpty couldn't be put together.

Page is blank for cutting exercise on previous page.

Name: _____

Comprehension: "Hey Diddle Diddle"

Directions: Read "Hey Diddle Diddle." Then answer the questions.

Hey diddle diddle,

The cat and the fiddle,

The cow jumped over the moon.

The little dog laughed

To see such sport,

And the dish ran away with the spoon!

1. Who jumped over the moon?

_____

----

2. Who laughed?

_____

----

3. Who ran away? _____ and _____

Comprehension: "Hey Diddle Diddle"

Directions: Read "Hey Diddle Diddle" again.
Then answer the questions.

1. What is a fiddle?

   _____

   -

   _____

2. What is another word for "jumped"?

   _____

   -

   _____

3. What word in the poem means the same as "giggled"?

   _____

   -

   _____

4. Where do you think the dish and the spoon went? Draw
   your answer.

Sequencing: "Hey Diddle Diddle"

Directions: Number the pictures for "Hey Diddle Diddle" in order.

Name: _____

Comprehension: "Bluebird"

Directions: Read the bluebird poem. Look at the picture. Write what the bluebird sees. Use words from the box.

Bluebird, bluebird,

Up in the tree,

How many blue things

Do you see?

book	flowers
girl	grass
hat	sky
shoes	tree

Here are the blue things the bluebird sees:

1. _____

2. _____   4. _____

3. _____   5. _____

Name: _____

Comprehension: "New Bird"

Directions: Fill in the blanks to create a poem about a different colored bird. Then draw a picture in the box to go with your poem.

_____ bird, _____ bird,

Up in the _____ ,

How many _____ things

Do you see?

_____

Directions: Fill in the blanks.

How many _____ things did the bird see in

your picture? _____

Sequencing: Make an Ice-Cream Cone

Directions: Number the boxes in order to show how to make an ice-cream cone.

Comprehension: Eating Ice Cream

Directions: Read the story. Write two things Sam could have done so he could have enjoyed eating his ice-cream cone.

It was a hot day. Sam went to the store and got an ice-cream cone. He ate it at a table in the sun. Sam watched some friends play ball. When he went to eat his ice-cream, it had melted and fallen on the sidewalk.

1. _____
_____

2. _____
_____

Sequencing: Eating a Cone

What if a person never ate an ice-cream cone? Could you tell them how to eat it? Think about what you do when you eat an ice-cream cone.

Directions: Write directions to teach someone how to eat an ice-cream cone.

How to Eat an Ice-Cream Cone

1. _____

2. _____

3. _____

4. _____

Name: _____

Review

Directions: Read about coins. Then answer the questions.

You can use coins to buy things. Some coins are worth more than others. Do you know these coins? A penny is worth one cent. A nickel is worth five cents. A dime is worth 10 cents. A quarter is worth 25 cents.

1. What can you use coins to do?

_____

- -

2. How are coins different?

_____

- -

Directions: Number the coins in order from the one that is worth the least to the one that is worth the most. Under each picture, write how many cents each coin is worth.

nickel ☐   penny ☐   dime ☐

- - - - - - - - - cents   - - - - - - - - - cent   - - - - - - - - - cents

Glossary

Abbreviation: A short way of writing words. Examples: **Mon.**, **Tues.**, etc.

Classifying: Putting objects, words or ideas that are alike into categories.

Comprehension: Understanding what is seen, heard or read.

Following Directions: Doing what the directions say to do.

Same and Different: Being able to tell how things are alike and not alike.

Sequencing: Putting things in order.

Answer Key

Comprehension: Snow Is Cold!

Directions: Read about snow. Circle the answers.

When you play in snow, dress warmly. Wear a coat. Wear a hat. Wear gloves. Do you wear these when you play in snow?

1. Snow is   warm. / (cold.)

2. When you play in snow, dress   (warmly.) / quickly.

Answers may include:

Directions: List three things to wear when you play in snow.

hat, scarf, gloves or mittens, coat, boots, snowpants, etc.

4

Same and Different

Directions: Circle five things in picture #1 that are not in picture #2.

#1

#2

5

Sequencing: Make a Snowman!

Directions: Write the number of the sentence that goes with each picture in the box.

1. Roll a large snowball for the snowman's bottom.
2. Make another snowball and put it on top of the first.
3. Put the last snowball on top.
4. Dress the snowman.

6

Classifying: What Does Not Belong?

Directions: Circle the two things that do not belong in the picture. Write why they do not belong.

1. Flowers do not grow in snow.
2. Palm trees do not grow in snow.

7

Classifying: These Keep Me Warm

Directions: Color the things that keep you warm.

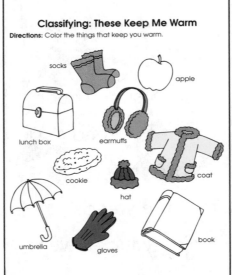

8

Comprehension: Raking Leaves

Directions: Read about raking leaves. Then answer the questions.

I like to rake leaves. Do you? Leaves die each year. They get brown and dry. They fall from the trees. Then we rake them up.

1. What color are leaves when they die?

brown

2. What happens when they die?

They get dry and fall from the tree.

3. What do we do when leaves fall?

We rake them.

9

Sequencing: Raking Leaves

Directions: Write a number in each box to show the order of the story.

10

Classifying: Leaves

Directions: Cut out the leaves. Put them into two groups. Glue each group in a box on the top of the page. Write a name for each group.

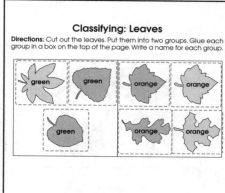

11

Comprehension: Growing Flowers

Directions: Read about flowers. Then write the answers.

Some flowers grow in pots. Many flowers grow in flower beds. Others grow beside the road. Flowers begin from seeds. They grow into small buds. Then they open wide and bloom. Flowers are pretty!

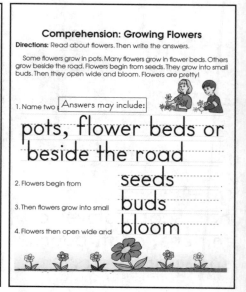

1. Name two Answers may include:

pots, flower beds or beside the road

2. Flowers begin from **seeds**

3. Then flowers grow into small **buds**

4. Flowers then open wide and **bloom**

13

Flower Puzzle

Directions: Read the story about flowers again. Then complete the puzzle.

Across:
2. Flowers do this when they open wide.
3. Flowers grow from these.

Down:
1. A flower can grow in a flower bed or a ___.
2. Before they bloom, flowers grow ___.

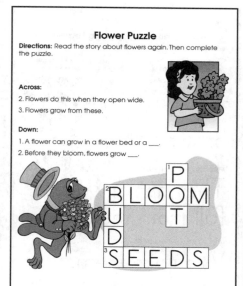

14

Sequencing: How Flowers Grow

Directions: Read the story. Then write the steps to grow a flower.

First find a sunny spot. Then plant the seed. Water it. The flower will start to grow. Pull the weeds around it. Remember to keep giving the flower water. Enjoy your flower.

1. Find a sunny spot
2. Plant the seed
3. Water it
4. Pull the weeds
5. Enjoy your flowers

15

Review

Directions: Write words in the blanks to make a label for a seed packet. Use ideas from the stories on pages 13 and 15 and your own ideas.

Flower Seeds

Plant seeds in a
bed or pot
Give them lots of
water
A bud will grow. Then it will
bloom
The flower will keep growing if you pull the
weeds around it.
Your flowers will be very **pretty**

16

Review

Directions: Read the story and look at the pictures. Then write the answers.

Some clothes are for winter. Some clothes are for summer. Winter clothes keep us warm. Summer clothes keep us cool. In summer, I put on shorts, then a shirt and then sandals. These clothes keep me cool!

shirt   scarf   coat   hat   sandals   shorts

1. Tell the order of clothes I put on in summer.

shorts   **shirt**   **sandals**
First   Then   Last

2. List the winter clothes pictured.

scarf   **coat**   **hat**

3. How are summer and winter clothes different?

Summer clothes keep us   Winter clothes keep us

cool   **warm**

17

Comprehension: Balloons

Directions: Read the story. Then answer the questions.

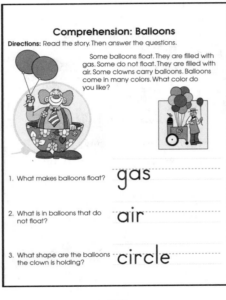

Some balloons float. They are filled with gas. Some do not float. They are filled with air. Some clowns carry balloons. Balloons come in many colors. What color do you like?

1. What makes balloons float?   **gas**

2. What is in balloons that do not float?   **air**

3. What shape are the balloons the clown is holding?   **circle**

18

Comprehension: Balloons

Directions: Read the story about balloons again. Draw a picture for the sentence in each box.

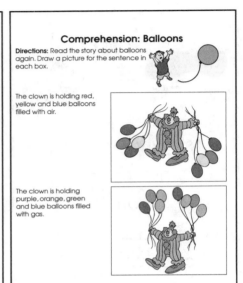

The clown is holding red, yellow and blue balloons filled with air.

The clown is holding purple, orange, green and blue balloons filled with gas.

19

Same and Different: Clowns

Directions: Look at the two clowns. Color the things in picture #2 that are different from the things in picture #1.

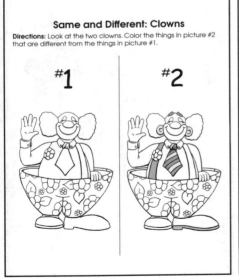

#1   #2

20

Following Directions: Color the Clown

Directions: Color the clown. Use your crayons this way: 1 = red, 2 = blue, 3 = orange, 4 = pink.

Directions: Write the answers on the lines.

1. What color did you use for the clown's hair?   **orange**

2. What color is the clown's nose?   **red**

3. What color is the clown's collar?   **blue**

4. What color is the clown's mouth?   **pink**

21

Classifying: Clowns and Balloons

Some words describe clowns. Some words describe balloons.

Directions: Read the words. Write the words that match in the correct columns.

float	laughs	hat	string
air	feet	pop	nose

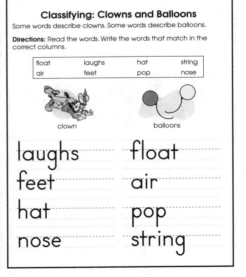

clown   balloons

laughs   **float**
feet   **air**
hat   **pop**
nose   **string**

22

Sequencing: Petting a Cat

Directions: Read the story. Then write the answers.

Do you like cats? I do. To pet a cat, move slowly. Hold out your hand. The cat will come to you. Then pet its head. Do not grab a cat! It will run away.

To pet a cat . . .

1. Move **slowly**

2. Hold our your **hand**

3. The cat will come to **you**

4. Pet the cat's **head**

5. Do not **grab**   a cat!

23

Comprehension: Cats

Directions: Read the story about cats again. Then write the answers.

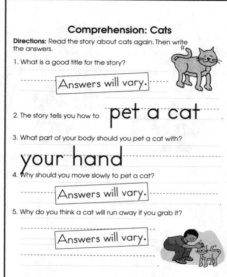

1. What is a good title for the story?

   Answers will vary.

2. The story tells you how to **pet a cat**

3. What part of your body should you pet a cat with?

   your hand

4. Why should you move slowly to pet a cat?

   Answers will vary.

5. Why do you think a cat will run away if you grab it?

   Answers will vary.

24

Comprehension: Cats

Directions: Look at the pictures and read about four cats. Then write the correct name beside each cat.

Fluffy, Blackie and Tiger are playing. Tom is sleeping. Blackie has spots. Tiger has stripes.

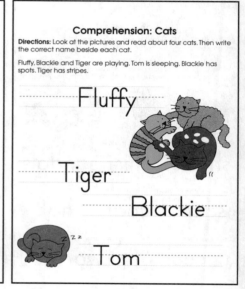

Fluffy

Tiger

Blackie

Tom

25

Same and Different: Cats

Directions: Compare the picture of the cats on page 25 to this picture. Write a word from the box to tell what is different about each cat.

| purple ball | green bow | blue brush | red collar |

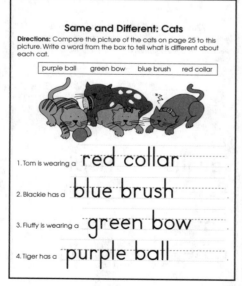

1. Tom is wearing a **red collar**

2. Blackie has a **blue brush**

3. Fluffy is wearing a **green bow**

4. Tiger has a **purple ball**

26

Comprehension: Tigers

Directions: Read about tigers. Then write the answers.

Tigers sleep during the day. They hunt at night. Tigers eat meat. They hunt deer. They like to eat wild pigs. If they cannot find meat, tigers will eat fish.

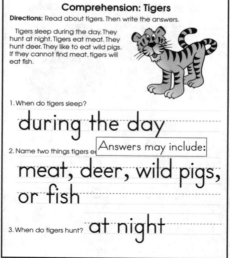

1. When do tigers sleep?

   during the day

2. Name two things tigers e   Answers may include:

   meat, deer, wild pigs, or fish

3. When do tigers hunt? **at night**

27

Following Directions: Tiger Puzzle

Directions: Read the story about tigers again. Then complete the puzzle.

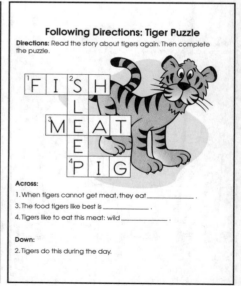

Crossword:
¹F I ²S H
    ³M E A T
      E
      ⁴P I G

Across:
1. When tigers cannot get meat, they eat _____ .
3. The food tigers like best is _____ .
4. Tigers like to eat this meat: wild _____ .

Down:
2. Tigers do this during the day.

28

Following Directions: Draw a Tiger

Directions: Follow directions to complete the picture of the tiger.

1. Draw black stripes on the tiger's body and tail.
2. Color the tiger's tongue red.
3. Draw claws on the feet.
4. Draw a black nose and two black eyes on the tiger's face.
5. Color the rest of the tiger orange.
6. Draw tall, green grass for the tiger to sleep in.

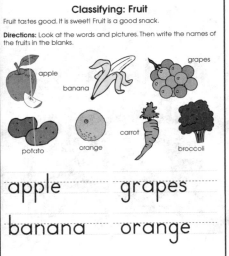

29

Review

Directions: Read about skiing. Circle the answers. Write a number in each box to show the order of the story.

Skiing Is Fun

You need to dress warmly to ski. One ski fits on each boot. You wear the skis to a chair called a ski lift. It takes you up in the air to a hill. When you get off, you ski down the hill. Be careful! Sometimes you will fall.

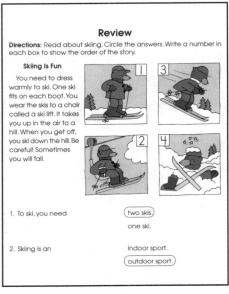

1. To ski, you need
   (two skis.)
   one ski.

2. Skiing is an
   indoor sport.
   (outdoor sport.)

30

Comprehension: Apples

Directions: Read about apples. Then write the answers.

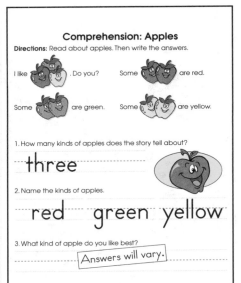

I like ___ . Do you?   Some ___ are red.

Some ___ are green.   Some ___ are yellow.

1. How many kinds of apples does the story tell about?

three

2. Name the kinds of apples.

red   green   yellow

3. What kind of apple do you like best?

Answers will vary.

31

Classifying: Fruit

Fruit tastes good. It is sweet! Fruit is a good snack.

Directions: Look at the words and pictures. Then write the names of the fruits in the blanks.

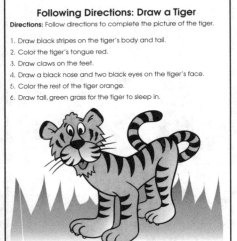

grapes
apple
banana
potato   orange   carrot   broccoli

apple   grapes

banana   orange

32

Classifying: Vegetables

Vegetables grow in gardens. Vegetables help keep us healthy.

Directions: Look at the pictures. Then write the name of the vegetables in the blanks.

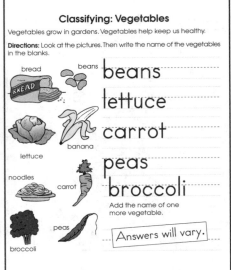

bread   beans   **beans**

lettuce

banana   **carrot**

lettuce   **peas**

noodles   carrot   **broccoli**

Add the name of one more vegetable.

Answers will vary.

broccoli   peas

33

Comprehension: How We Eat

Directions: Read the story. Use words from the box to answer the questions.

People eat with spoons and forks. They use a spoon to eat soup and ice cream. They use a fork to eat potatoes. They use a knife to cut their meat. They say, "Thank you. It was good!" when they finish.

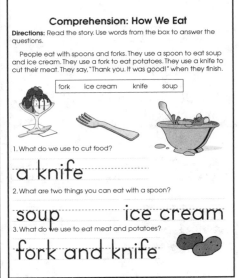

| fork | ice cream | knife | soup |

1. What do we use to cut food?

a knife

2. What are two things you can eat with a spoon?

soup   ice cream

3. What do we use to eat meat and potatoes?

fork and knife

34

Classifying: Foods

Directions: Read the questions under each plate. Draw three foods on each plate to answer the questions.

1. What foods can you cut with a knife?

2. What foods should you eat with a fork?

3. What foods can you eat with a spoon?

35

Comprehension: Familiar Objects

Directions: Write each word next to its picture in the puzzle.

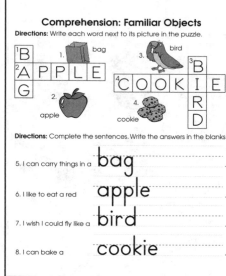

bag

1.

bird

apple

cookie

Directions: Complete the sentences. Write the answers in the blanks.

5. I can carry things in a   bag

6. I like to eat a red   apple

7. I wish I could fly like a   bird

8. I can bake a   cookie

36

Classifying: Things That Belong Together

Directions: Circle the pictures in each row that belong together.

Row 1   knife   key   fork   spoon

Row 2   orange   apple   candy   banana

Row 3   beach ball   soccer ball   baseball   apple

Directions: Write the names of the pictures that do not belong.

Row 1   key

Row 2   candy

Row 3   apple

37

Classifying: Why They Are Different

Directions: Look at your answers on page 37. Write why each object does not belong.

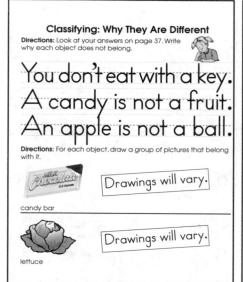

You don't eat with a key.
A candy is not a fruit.
An apple is not a ball.

Directions: For each object, draw a group of pictures that belong with it.

Drawings will vary.

candy bar

Drawings will vary.

lettuce

38

Comprehension: Write a Party Invitation

Directions: Read about the party. Then complete the invitation.

The party will be at Dog's house. The party will start at 1:00 P.M. It will last 2 hours. Write your birthday for the date of the party.

Party Invitation

Where: Dog's house

Date: Answers will vary.

Time It Begins: 1:00 P.M.

Time It Ends: 3:00 P.M.

Answers will vary.

Directions: On the last line, write something else about the party.

39

Sequencing: Pig Gets Ready

Directions: Number the pictures of Pig getting ready for the party to show the order of the story.

What kind of party do you think Pig is going to?   Answers will vary.

40

Comprehension: An Animal Party

Directions: Use the picture for clues. Write words from the box to answer the questions.

bear	cat
dog	elephant
giraffe	hippo
pig	tiger

1. Which animals have bow ties?

cat   tiger

2. Which animal has a hat?

bear

3. Which animal has a striped shirt?

pig

41

Classifying: Party Items

Directions: Draw a ☐ around objects that are food for the party. Draw a △ around the party guests. Draw a ◯ around the objects used for fun at the party.

ice cream   candy   games   tiger

noise makers   cake   garbage can   cat   hat

glasses   candle   bear   juice   balloons

giraffe   pig   potato chips   hippo

42

Review

Directions: Read about cookies. Then write your answers.

Cookies are made with many things. All cookies are made with flour. Some cookies have nuts in them. Some cookies do not. Some cookies have chocolate chips. Some do not. Cookbooks give directions on how to make cookies.

First, turn on the oven. Then get out all the things that go in the cookies. Mix them together. Roll them out, and cut the cookies. Bake the cookies. Now eat them!

1. Tell one way all cookies are the same.

All cookies are made with flour.

2. Name one different thing in cookie

Answers may include:

nuts or chocolate chips

3. Where do you find directions for making cookies?

in cookbooks

43

Comprehension: The Teddy Bear Song

Do you know the Teddy Bear Song? It is very old!

Directions: Read the Teddy Bear Song. Then answer the questions.

Teddy bear, teddy bear, turn around.
Teddy bear, teddy bear, touch the ground.
Teddy bear, teddy bear, climb upstairs.
Teddy bear, teddy bear, say your prayers.
Teddy bear, teddy bear, turn out the light.
Teddy bear, teddy bear, say, "Good night!"

1. What is the first thing the teddy bear does?

He turns around.

2. What is the last thing the teddy bear does?

He says, "Good night!"

3. What would you name a teddy bear?

Answers will vary.

44

Following Directions: Make a Teddy Bear

Directions: Color and cut out the teddy bear. Act out the song on page 44 with your teddy bear.

Colors will vary.

45

Comprehension: A New Teddy Bear Song

Directions: Write words to make a new teddy bear song. Act out your new song with your teddy bear as you read it.

Answers will vary.

Teddy bear, teddy bear, turn

Teddy bear, teddy bear, touch the

Teddy bear, teddy bear, climb

Teddy bear, teddy bear, turn out

Teddy bear, teddy bear, say,

47

Sequencing: Put Teddy Bear to Bed

Directions: Read the song about the teddy bear again. Write a number in each box to show the order of the story.

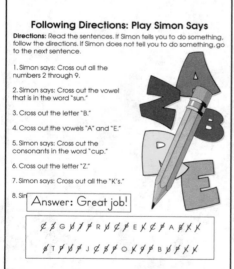

48

Comprehension: Play Simon Says

Directions: Read how to play Simon Says. Then answer the questions.

Simon Says

Here is how to play Simon Says: One kid is Simon. Simon is the leader. Everyone must do what Simon says and does but only if the leader says, "Simon says" first. Let's try it. "Simon says, 'Pat your head.'" "Simon says, 'Pat your nose. Pat your toes.'" Oops! Did you pat your toes? I did not say, "Simon says," first. If you patted your toes, you are out!

1. Who is the leader in this game? Simon

2. What must the leader say first each time? "Simon says"

3. What happens if you do something and the leader did not say, "Simon says?" You are out.

49

Comprehension: Play Simon Says

Directions: Read each sentence. Look at the picture next to it. Circle the picture if the person is playing Simon Says correctly.

1. Simon says, "Put your hands on your hips."
2. Simon says, "Stand on one leg."
3. Simon says, "Put your hands on your head."
4. Simon says, "Ride a bike."
5. Simon says, "Jump up and down."
6. Simon says, "Pet a dog."
7. Simon says, "Make a big smile."

50

Following Directions: Play Simon Says

Directions: Read the sentences. If Simon tells you to do something, follow the directions. If Simon does not tell you to do something, go to the next sentence.

1. Simon says: Cross out all the numbers 2 through 9.
2. Simon says: Cross out the vowel that is in the word "sun."
3. Cross out the letter "B."
4. Cross out the vowels "A" and "E."
5. Simon says: Cross out the consonants in the word "cup."
6. Cross out the letter "Z."
7. Simon says: Cross out all the "K's."
8. Sim

Answer: Great job!

51

Same and Different: Look at Simon

Directions: Find four things in picture #2 that are not in picture #1. Write your answers. Use words from the box.

| hat | head | socks | bare feet |
| feather | watch | untied shoes | shirt |

1. feather
2. socks
3. watch
4. untied shoes

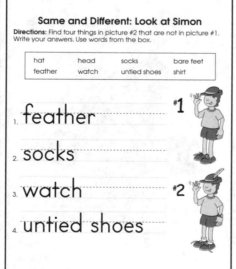

52

Comprehension: Crayons

Directions: Read about crayons. Then write your answers.

Crayons come in many colors. Some crayons are dark colors. Some crayons are light colors. All crayons have wax in them.

1. How many colors of crayons are there? many / few
2. Crayons come in dark colors and light colors.
3. What do all crayons have in them? They have wax in them.

53

Following Directions: Hidden Picture

Directions: To find the hidden picture, color only the shapes with a number inside.

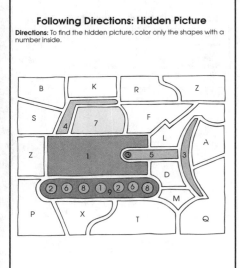

54

Comprehension: Rhymes

Directions: Read about words that rhyme. Then circle the answers.

Words that rhyme have the same end sounds. "Wing" and "sing" rhyme. "Boy" and "toy" rhyme. "Dime" and "time" rhyme. Can you think of other words that rhyme?

1. Words that rhyme have the same ⟨end sounds.⟩ / end letters.

2. "Time" rhymes with "tree." / ⟨"dime."⟩

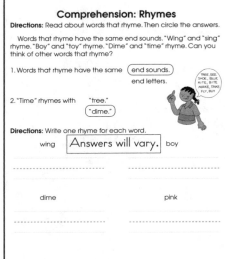

TREE, SEE, SHOE, BLUE, KITE, BITE, MAKE, TAKE, FLY, BUY

Directions: Write one rhyme for each word.

wing   Answers will vary.   boy

_____   _____

dime   pink

_____   _____

55

Classifying: Rhymes

Directions: Circle the pictures in each row that rhyme.

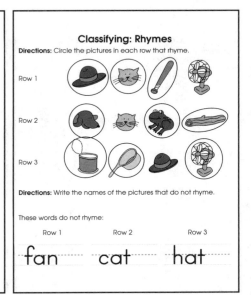

Row 1

Row 2

Row 3

Directions: Write the names of the pictures that do not rhyme.

These words do not rhyme:

Row 1   Row 2   Row 3

fan   cat   hat

56

Classifying: Rhymes

Directions: Cut out the pieces. Read the words. Find two words that rhyme. Put the words together.

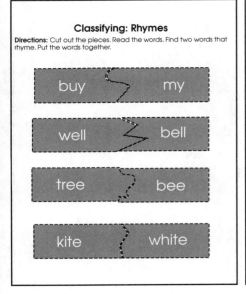

buy   my

well   bell

tree   bee

kite   white

57

Review

Directions: Read about ways you move. Circle the correct answer.

You can move in many ways. You can run. When you run, one foot hits the ground at a time. You can jump. When you jump, you land on two feet. You can hop. To hop, first stand on one leg. Then jump up and down.

1. Running and jumping are different because

A) One foot hits the ground at a time when you run. Two feet hit the ground at a time when you jump.

OR

B) Two feet hit the ground at a time when you run. One foot hits the ground at a time when you jump.

Directions: Write directions on how to hop.

2. First, stand on one leg

3. Then, jump up and down

59

Comprehension: Babies

Directions: Read about babies. Then write the answers.

Babies are small. Some babies cry a lot. They cry when they are wet. They cry when they are hungry. They smile when they are dry. They smile when they are fed.

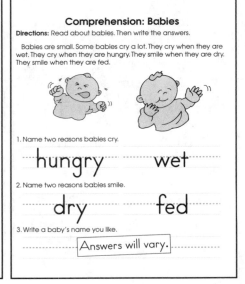

1. Name two reasons babies cry.

hungry   wet

2. Name two reasons babies smile.

dry   fed

3. Write a baby's name you like.

_____ Answers will vary. _____

60

Comprehension: Babies

Directions: Read each sentence. Draw a picture of a baby's face in the box to show if she would cry or smile.

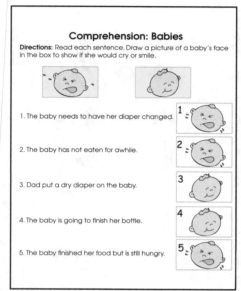

1. The baby needs to have her diaper changed.
2. The baby has not eaten for awhile.
3. Dad put a dry diaper on the baby.
4. The baby is going to finish her bottle.
5. The baby finished her food but is still hungry.

61

Sequencing: Feeding Baby

Directions: Read the sentences. Write a number in each box to show the order of the story.

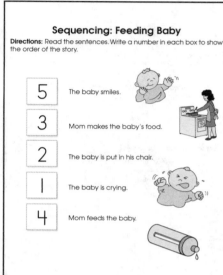

5   The baby smiles.

3   Mom makes the baby's food.

2   The baby is put in his chair.

1   The baby is crying.

4   Mom feeds the baby.

62

Same and Different: Compare the Twins

Directions: Read the story. Then use the words in the box and the picture to write your answers.

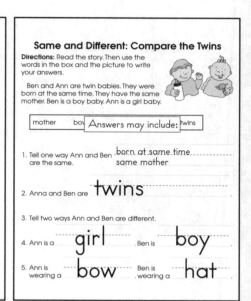

Ben and Ann are twin babies. They were born at the same time. They have the same mother. Ben is a boy baby. Ann is a girl baby.

| mother | boy | Answers may include: | twins |

1. Tell one way Ann and Ben are the same.   born at same time / same mother

2. Anna and Ben are   twins

3. Tell two ways Ann and Ben are different.

4. Ann is a   girl   . Ben is   boy

5. Ann is wearing a   bow   . Ben is wearing a   hat

63

Comprehension: Hats

Directions: Read about hats. Then write your answers.

There are many kinds of hats. Some baseball hats have brims. Some fancy hats have feathers. Some knit hats pull down over your ears. Some hats are made of straw. Do you like hats?

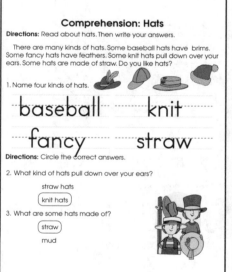

1. Name four kinds of hats.

baseball   knit

fancy   straw

Directions: Circle the correct answers.

2. What kind of hats pull down over your ears?

  straw hats
  (knit hats)

3. What are some hats made of?

  (straw)
  mud

64

Sequencing: Choosing a Hat

Directions: Write a number in each box to show the order of the story.

1   4
3   2

65

Classifying: Hats

Directions: A store has four types of hats. Draw three hats for each type listed. Write what kind of hats you think should be in the last group, and draw three of that kind.

Drawings will vary.

Tall Hats   Hats With Points

Fancy Hats

66

Classifying: Mr. Lincoln's Hat

Abraham Lincoln wore a tall hat. He liked to keep things in his hat so he would not lose them.

Directions: Cut out the pictures of things Mr. Lincoln could have kept in his hat. Glue those pictures on the hat.

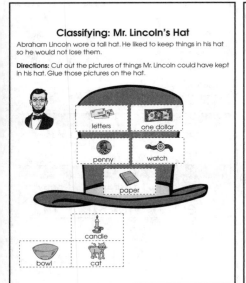

67

Following Directions: Draw Hats

Directions: Draw a hat on each person. Read the sentences to know what kind of hat to draw.

1. The first girl is wearing a purple hat with feathers.

2. The boy next to the girl with the purple hat is wearing a red baseball hat.

3. The first boy is wearing a yellow knit hat.

4. The last boy is wearing a brown top hat.

5. The girl next to the boy with the red hat is wearing a blue straw hat.

69

Review

Directions: Read the story. Then circle the pictures of things that are wet.

Some things used in baking are dry. Some things used in baking are wet. To bake a cake, first mix the salt, sugar and flour. Then add the egg. Now, add the milk. Stir. Put the cake in the oven.

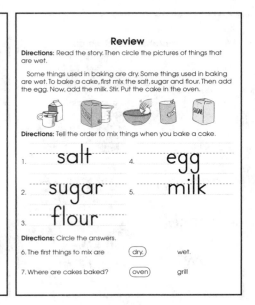

Directions: Tell the order to mix things when you bake a cake.

1. salt   4. egg
2. sugar   5. milk
3. flour

Directions: Circle the answers.

6. The first things to mix are   (dry.)   wet.

7. Where are cakes baked?   (oven)   grill

70

Following Directions: Complete the Puzzle

Directions: Read the story. Then complete the puzzle.

The Zoo and the Farm

The zoo is for wild animals. Tigers live at the zoo. Some snakes live at the zoo. The farm is for tame animals. Ducks and donkeys live on farms.

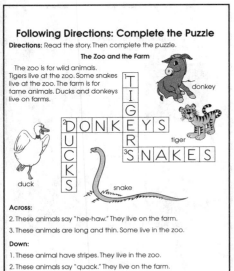

Across:

2. These animals say "hee-haw." They live on the farm.

3. These animals are long and thin. Some live in the zoo.

Down:

1. These animal have stripes. They live in the zoo.

2. These animals say "quack." They live on the farm.

71

Comprehension: Farm Sounds

Directions: Read the story. Then answer the questions.

You can hear many sounds on the farm. Roosters crow in the morning. The cows moo, and donkeys say, "hee-haw." You might even hear the tractor motor humming.

1. What animal crows in the morning?   rooster

2. What sound does the cow make?   moo

3. This thing is not an animal?   tractor

4. What animal says "hee-haw"?   donkey

Directions: Circle the farm words in the puzzle. Look up and down and sideways.

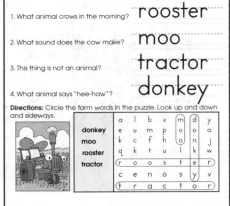

72

Same and Different: Compare the Barnyards

Directions: Look at the pictures of the barnyards. Color the five things in picture #1 that are different from picture #2.

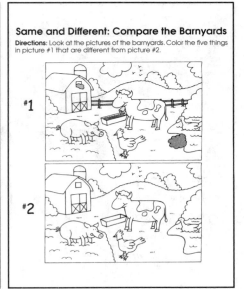

73

Comprehension: Animals

Directions: Read about inside and outside animals. Circle the pictures of animals that can live inside.

Some animals belong inside. Some animals belong outside. Wild animals belong outside. Large animals belong outside. Small, tame animals can live inside.

Directions: Write the names of animals that belong outside.

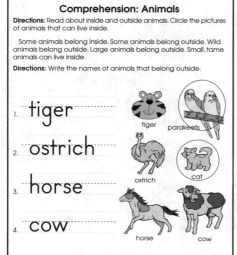

1. tiger
2. ostrich
3. horse
4. cow

tiger
parakeets
ostrich
cat
horse
cow

Comprehension: Days

Directions: Read about the days of the week. Then answer the questions.

Do you know the names of the seven days of the week? Here they are: Sunday, Monday, Tuesday, Wednesday, Thursday, Friday and Saturday.

1. What day comes after Thursday?

Friday

2. What day comes before Tuesday?

Monday

3. How many days are in each week?

seven

Following Directions: Days of the Week

Calendars show the days of the week in order. Sunday comes first. Saturday comes last. There are five days in between. An **abbreviation** is a short way of writing words. The abbreviations for the days of the week are usually the first three or four letters of the word followed by a period.

Example: Sunday — Sun.

Directions: Write the days of the week in order on the calendar. Use the abbreviations.

Day 1	Day 2	Day 3
Sunday	Monday	Tuesday
Sun.	Mon.	Tues.
Day 4	Day 5	Day 6
Wednesday	Thursday	Friday
Wed.	Thurs.	Fri.
	Day 7	
	Saturday	
	Sat.	

74

75

76

Comprehension: Boats

Directions: Read about boats. Then answer the questions.

See the boats! They float on water. Some boats have sails. The wind moves the sails. It makes the boats go. Many people name their sailboats. They paint the name on the side of the boat.

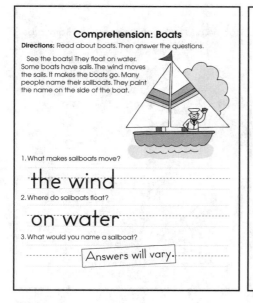

1. What makes sailboats move?

the wind

2. Where do sailboats float?

on water

3. What would you name a sailboat?

Answers will vary.

Same and Different: Color the Boats

Directions: Find the three boats that are alike. Color them all the same. One boat is different. Color it differently.

Comprehension: A Boat Ride

Directions: Write a sentence under each picture to tell what is happening. Read the story you wrote.

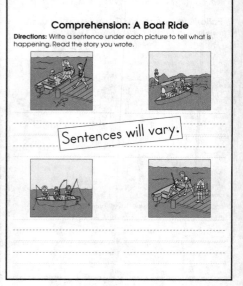

Sentences will vary.

77

78

79

Comprehension: Travel

Directions: Read the story. Then answer the questions.

Let's Take a Trip!

Pack your bag. Shall we go by car, plane or train? Let's go to the sea. When we get there, let's go on a sailboat.

1. What are three ways to travel?

Answer may also include sailboat

car   plane   train

2. Where will we go?

Answers will vary.

3. What will we do when we get there?

Answers will vary.

80

Following Directions: Draw a Path

Directions: Read about how to get to the beach. Use a crayon to draw the way to the beach.

Let's Go to the Beach

On the way to the beach, you will stop for food, then gas. Next, you cross a bridge. Finally, you will be at the beach!

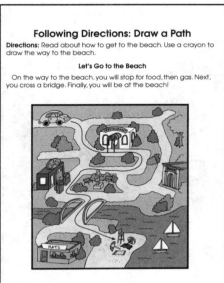

81

Review

Directions: Read the story. Then write the answers.

Fun With Balls

Some balls are soft. A beach ball is soft. Some balls are hard. We play baseball with a hard ball. Basketballs bounce. Can you throw a basketball through a hoop? First, bounce it three times. Then hold the basketball high. Now, throw it toward the hoop. Did you make a basket?

1. Tell how to throw a basketball.

First, bounce it three times

Second, hold the basketball high

Then throw it toward the hoop

2. How is a beach ball different from a hard ball?

It is soft.

82

Comprehension: Clocks

Directions: Read about clocks. Then answer the questions.

Ticking Clocks

Many clocks make two sounds. The sounds are tick and tock. Big clocks often make loud tick-tocks. Little clocks often make quiet tick-tocks. Sometimes people put little clocks in a box with a new puppy. The puppy likes the sound. The tick-tock makes the puppy feel safe.

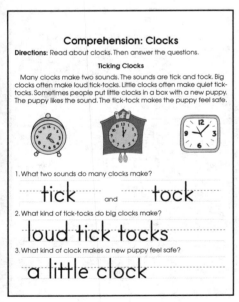

1. What two sounds do many clocks make?

tick   and   tock

2. What kind of tick-tocks do big clocks make?

loud tick tocks

3. What kind of clock makes a new puppy feel safe?

a little clock

83

Sequencing: Help the Puppy Feel Safe

Directions: Read the story about clocks again. Then write a number in each box to show the order of the story.

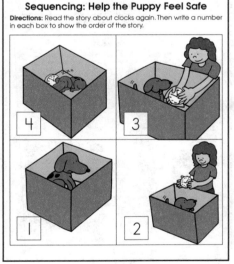

84

Same and Different: These Don't Belong

Directions: Circle the pictures in each row that go together.

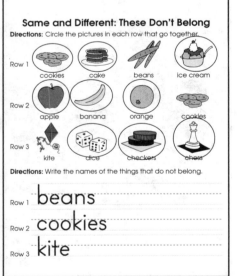

Row 1   cookies   cake   beans   ice cream

Row 2   apple   banana   orange   cookies

Row 3   kite   dice   checkers   chess

Directions: Write the names of the things that do not belong.

Row 1   beans

Row 2   cookies

Row 3   kite

85

Classifying: Things to Drink

Directions: Circle the pictures of things you can drink. Write the names of those things in the blanks.

milk
ice
soup and crackers
juice
soda
ice-cream bar

milk

juice   soda

86

Classifying: Things to Chew

Directions: Draw a line from the pictures of things you chew to the plate.

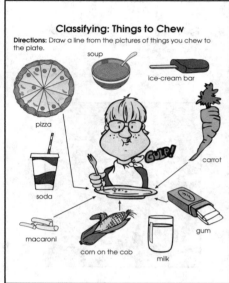

soup
ice-cream bar
pizza
carrot
GULP!
soda
macaroni
corn on the cob
gum
milk

87

Comprehension: Soup

Directions: Read about soup. Then write the answers.

I Like Soup

Soup is good! It is good for you, too. We eat most kinds of soup hot. Some people eat cold soup in the summer. Carrots and beans are in some soups. Do you like crackers with soup?

1. Name two ways people eat soup.

cold   hot

2. Name two things that are in some soups.

carrots   beans

3. Name the kind of soup you like best.

Answers will vary.

88

Same and Different: Soup

Directions: Circle the five things in picture #1 that are not in picture #2.

#1   #2

89

Comprehension: The Three Bears

Directions: Read about the three bears. Put #1 beside Papa Bear's bed. Put #2 beside Mama Bear's bed. Put #3 beside Baby Bear's bed.

The Three Bears

Do you know the story of the three bears? Papa Bear is the biggest bear. He has the biggest bed. Mama Bear is a middle-size bear. She has a middle-size bed. Baby Bear is the little bear. He has the smallest bed.

#1   #2   1
3
#3   2

90

Comprehension: The Three Bears

Directions: Draw the objects that belong to the three bears. Then complete the sentences. Draw the bowls.

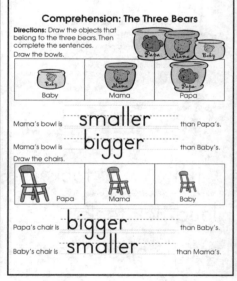

Papa Mama Baby
Baby   Mama   Papa

Mama's bowl is **smaller** than Papa's.

Mama's bowl is **bigger** than Baby's.

Draw the chairs.

Papa   Mama   Baby

Papa's chair is **bigger** than Baby's.

Baby's chair is **smaller** than Mama's.

91

Following Directions: Three Bears Puzzle

Directions: Read the story about the three bears again. Then complete the puzzle.

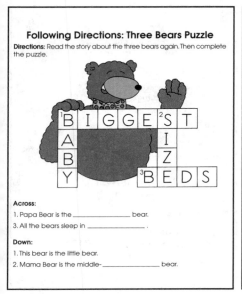

```
¹B I G G E ²S T
A       I
B       Z
Y     ³B E D S
```

Across:

1. Papa Bear is the _____ bear.
3. All the bears sleep in _____ .

Down:

1. This bear is the little bear.
2. Mama Bear is the middle-_____ bear.

92

Review

Directions: Read how to make no-cook candy. Then answer the questions.

Some candy needs to be cooked on a stove. You do not need to cook this kind of candy. It is easy to make. You will need a large bowl for mixing. You will need five things to make this candy.

No-Cook Candy
½ cup peanut butter
4 cups powdered sugar
1 cup cocoa
pinch of salt
4 tablespoons milk

Mix everything in the bowl. Roll it into small balls. (A pinch of salt is just a tiny bit.)

1. What is third on the list of things needed?

I cup cocoa

2. What is different about no-cook candy?

You don't have to cook it.
Roll it into small balls.

93

Comprehension: "Humpty Dumpty"

Directions: Read the poem. Draw a picture of Humpty Dumpty after he fell off the wall.

Humpty Dumpty sat on a wall.
Humpty Dumpty had a great fall.
All the king's horses and all the king's men
Couldn't put Humpty together again.

Drawings will vary.

94

Sequencing: Put Humpty Together

Directions: Cut out the pieces and mix them up. Then read the sentence on each piece to put Humpty back together.

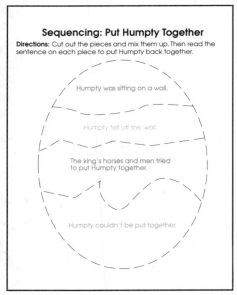

Humpty was sitting on a wall.

Humpty fell off the wall.

The king's horses and men tried to put Humpty together.

1

Humpty couldn't be put together.

95

Comprehension: "Hey Diddle Diddle"

Directions: Read "Hey Diddle Diddle." Then answer the questions.

Hey diddle diddle,
The cat and the fiddle,
The cow jumped over the moon.
The little dog laughed
To see such sport,
And the dish ran away with the spoon!

1. Who jumped over the moon?

the cow

2. Who laughed?

the little dog

3. Who ran away?   dish and spoon

97

Comprehension: "Hey Diddle Diddle"

Directions: Read "Hey Diddle Diddle" again. Then answer the questions.

1. What is a fiddle?

a musical instrument

2. What is another word for "jump"? Answers may include:

hopped, leapt, etc.

3. What word in the poem means the same as "giggled"?

laughed

4. Where do you think the dish and the spoon went? Draw your answer.

Drawings will vary.

98

Sequencing: "Hey Diddle Diddle"

Directions: Number the pictures for "Hey Diddle Diddle" in order.

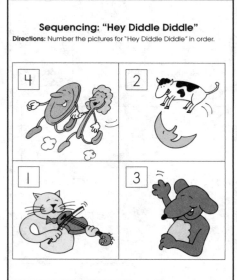

99

Comprehension: "Bluebird"

Directions: Read the bluebird poem. Look at the picture. Write what the bluebird sees. Use words from the box.

Bluebird, bluebird,
Up in the tree,
How many blue things
Do you see?

book	flowers
girl	grass
hat	sky
shoes	tree

Here are the blue things the bluebird sees:

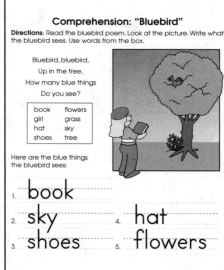

1. book
2. sky
3. shoes
4. hat
5. flowers

100

Comprehension: "New Bird"

Directions: Fill in the blanks to create a poem about a different colored bird. Then draw a picture in the box to go with your poem.

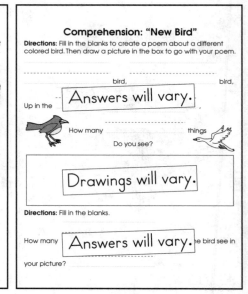

_____ bird, _____ bird,

Up in the [Answers will vary.]

How many _____ things

Do you see?

[Drawings will vary.]

Directions: Fill in the blanks.

How many [Answers will vary.] he bird see in your picture?

101

Sequencing: Make an Ice-Cream Cone

Directions: Number the boxes in order to show how to make an ice-cream cone.

102

Comprehension: Eating Ice Cream

Directions: Read the story. Write two things Sam could have done so he could have enjoyed eating his ice-cream cone.

It was a hot day. Sam went to the store and got an ice-cream cone. He ate it at a table in the sun. Sam watched some friends play ball. When he went to eat his ice-cream, it had melted and fallen on the sidewalk.

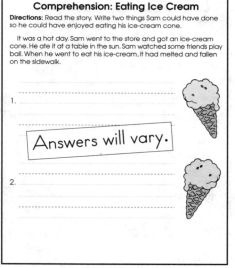

1. _____

[Answers will vary.]

2. _____

103

Sequencing: Eating a Cone

What if a person never ate an ice-cream cone? Could you tell them how to eat it? Think about what you do when you eat an ice-cream cone.

Directions: Write directions to teach someone how to eat an ice-cream cone.

How to Eat an Ice-Cream Cone

1.

2. Answers will vary.

3.

4.

Review

Directions: Read about coins. Then answer the questions.

You can use coins to buy things. Some coins are worth more than others. Do you know these coins? A penny is worth one cent. A nickel is worth five cents. A dime is worth 10 cents. A quarter is worth 25 cents.

1. What can you use coins to do?

You can use coins to buy things.

2. How are coins different?

Answers will vary.

Directions: Number the coins in order from the one that is worth the least to the one that is worth the most. Under each picture, write how many cents each coin is worth.

nickel [2]   penny [1]   dime [3]

five cents   one cent   ten cents

104

105

Teaching Suggestions

The goal of reading is to understand what is read. In addition to saying the words, your child needs to comprehend what the words are telling him/her. Learning skills such as classifying, comprehension, following directions, recognizing similarities and differences and sequencing will help your child become a better reader. You can use the ideas on these pages to help your child master these skills.

Classifying

Classifying involves putting objects, words or ideas that are alike into categories. Items can be classified in more than one way. For example, hats could be sorted by size, color or season worn. If your child creates a category you had not considered, praise him/her for thinking creatively.

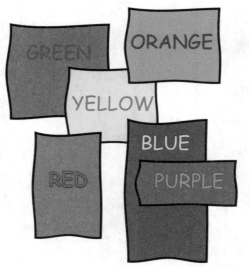

Your child could sort the clothing in his/her closet. He/she could sort it according to the season each item is worn, by color, type of clothing or even likes and dislikes. You can have your child help you sort laundry by colors.

At the grocery store, talk about the layout of the store and how items are arranged in the store. For example, fruits are together, vegetables are together, cooking supplies are together, soups are together, etc. Talk about why items would be arranged in groups like that. What would happen if they were not arranged in groups?

Have your child help you find what you need by having him/her decide what section of the store it would be in. After finding the item, talk about alternate places the item could be found.

When planning a family vacation, collect travel brochures on possible destinations and sites to see. Have your child classify the brochures according to location, activity or places you may or may not want to visit. Use these groupings to plan your trip.

Comprehension

Comprehension involves understanding what is seen, heard or read. To help your child with this skill, talk about a book, picture, movie or television program. Ask your child if he/she likes it and the reasons why or why not. By listening to what he/she says, you can tell whether the book, etc. was understood. If your child does not fully understand part of it, discuss that section further. Reread the book or watch the program again, if possible.

Your child can make a poster for a book or movie. Have him/her include the important events, most exciting parts, favorite part and reasons why someone else should view or read it.

Watch the news with your child and discuss the job of a news reporter. After your child understands what reporters do, create your own newscast. You can be the reporter, and your child can pretend to be a character from a book or movie. Make up the questions together, based on a book read or movie watched. Use the questions for an "interview." If you have a video camera, record your interview, and play it back for your child to watch.

After reading a book, have your child create a book cover for it. The picture should tell about the book and include a brief summary on the back. If the book belongs to your child, he/she could use the cover on the book.

Find a cartoon without words or cut a cartoon from the newspaper and cut off the words. Have your child look at the pictures and create words to go along with the pictures. If your child has difficulty writing, you can write what he/she says.

Following Directions

Cooking is one of many daily activities that involves following directions. Whether it is heating a can of soup, cooking a frozen dinner or making a box of pudding, all involve following directions. Read the package directions with your child and have him/her help you.

When you have a shelving unit, table, toy, etc. to assemble, allow your child to help. Point to each step in the directions. Read each step out loud together. Then follow the steps in order.

Like following package directions or a recipe, assembling an item enables your child to see that following directions is a skill used in every day situations.

Building a model and making craft projects are other ways for your child to learn to follow directions. Rather than a store-bought model, you could make your own by precutting wood pieces to make a birdhouse or other small item. Write step-by-step directions for your child. Then use the directions with your child to actually make it.

Each day, make a list of the jobs your child needs to complete. Then your child can follow the list to complete the jobs. If your child has difficulty reading, you can draw small pictures to represent each job. You know your child is able to follow directions when tasks are completed correctly.

Same and Different

This skill involves being able to tell how things are alike and not alike. This can easily be incorporated into daily activities. For instance, when driving in a car, have your child compare objects seen, such as cars and trucks, telling how they are the same and how they are different.

At home or in the grocery store, compare foods such as green apples and pears or broccoli and beans asking your child for ideas about how they are the same and different. Your child can also compare the taste and texture of the foods.

When shopping for clothes, ask your child how two shirts, pairs of pants or shoes look the same and different. Then if your child tries them on, he/she can compare how they fit.

Outside, your child can compare types of flowers or trees. Besides the physical characteristics like color, size and smell, also compare the needs of plants, such as water, sun and soil.

Your child can compare objects verbally or create a chart to record the similarities and differences. He/she can make lists that show objects that are the same and different.

Sequencing

Sequencing involves putting things in order. This can include steps to complete a task, sizes of objects or the time events occur during the day. To help your child with sequencing, get a comic strip that has three or four sections and read it with your child. Cut the sections apart and then have your child put it back together. If this is too difficult for your child, use a strip with only two sections at first.

In the morning, tell your child three steps involved in making his/her bed. Have your child tell you the order of the steps and then actually make the bed. At the end of the day, your child can put away the toys in a specific order, such as from smallest to largest or lightest to heaviest.

Have your child keep a journal. This not only helps with sequencing, but it is a good way to record what is happening in his/her life for the future. Each night in the journal, have your child write or draw four things that he/she did during the day.